A TREASURY OF
STENCIL DESIGNS
FOR ARTISTS AND CRAFTSMEN

Edited and with an Introduction by
Martin J. Isaacson and Dorothy A. Rennie

Dover Publications, Inc., New York

Copyright © 1976 by Dover Publications, Inc.
All rights reserved under Pan American and International Copyright Conventions.

Published in Canada by General Publishing Company, Ltd., 30 Lesmill Road, Don Mills, Toronto, Ontario.

Published in the United Kingdom by Constable and Company, Ltd.

A Treasury of Stencil Designs for Artists and Craftsmen is a new work, first published by Dover Publications, Inc. in 1976.

DOVER *Pictorial Archive* SERIES

This book belongs to the Dover Pictorial Archive Series. You may use the designs and illustrations for graphics and crafts applications, free and without special permission, provided that you include no more than ten in the same publication or project. (For permission for additional use, please write to Dover Publications, Inc., 31 East 2nd Street, Mineola, N.Y. 11501.)

However, republication or reproduction of any illustration by any other graphic service whether it be in a book or in any other design resource is strictly prohibited.

International Standard Book Number: 0-486-23307-3
Library of Congress Catalog Card Number: 75-46105

Manufactured in the United States of America
Dover Publications, Inc.
31 East 2nd Street
Mineola, N.Y. 11501

Introduction

The designs in this book are all taken from stencils used to decorate the interiors of Pennsylvania Railroad passenger coaches between 1924 and 1934, when the company, in the face of increasing competition from bus and car, was seeking an inexpensive means for making its services more attractive to the broader public. The designs come from the collection of Edward H. Bowers, a designer and painter employed at the railroad's paint shops in Altoona, Pennsylvania. Most of them are taken from the notebook in which he recorded the stencil designs he used. The others are reproduced from actual stencils which were not recorded in the notebook, though they had been in his possession. Composed principally of floral and geometric patterns of varying complexity, the collection forms an unusually large and handsome decorative ensemble which can be used for many purposes and in various media.

Little is known about Bowers. In 1890, at the age of 20, he was hired by the railroad as an office clerk. In 1895 he requested and was granted a transfer to the paint shops, where he remained until his retirement in June, 1941. He died in December of the same year. In 1933, when the railroads were feeling the effect of the Depression, he had proposed a program of extensive redecoration of the company's passenger cars, but finances were too limited and the plan was never adopted.

Bowers probably received his training as a designer with the railroad; it was customary for junior employees to serve an apprenticeship of several years. The original design source material that he left behind attests to his interest in both Victorian and Art Nouveau decorative art. French, German and English motifs were found with his collection of stencils, as well as suggestions for artists by Dominic M. Campana, an Italian-American who created designs for the Lenox China Company at the turn of the century. While these influences can be seen in Bowers' work, his designs reflect his own artistic imagination and craft.

MARTIN J. ISAACSON
DOROTHY A. RENNIE

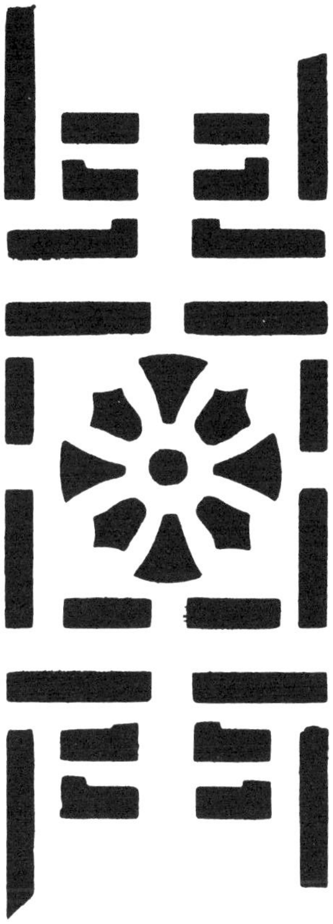

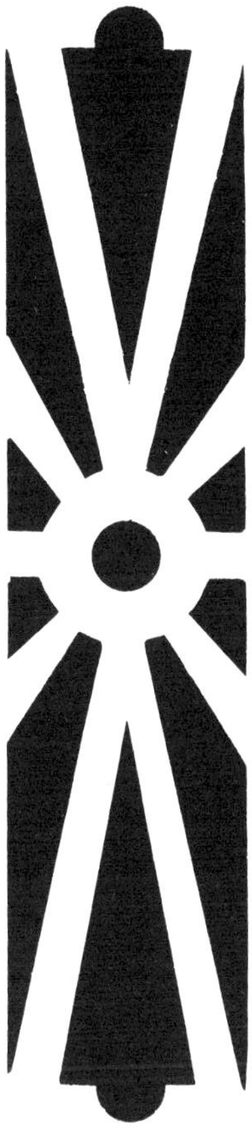

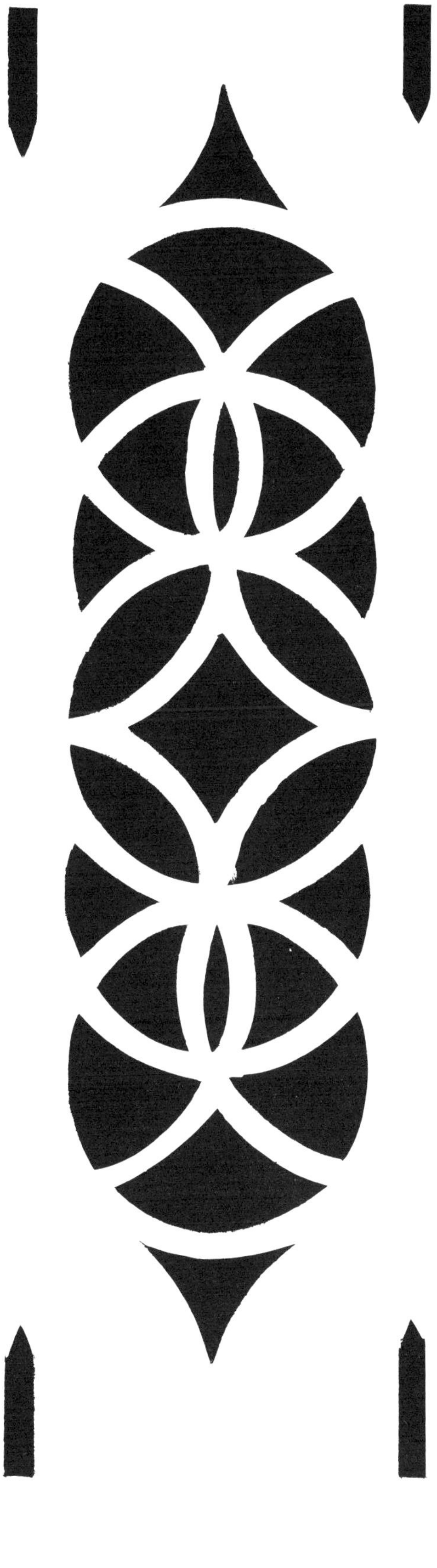

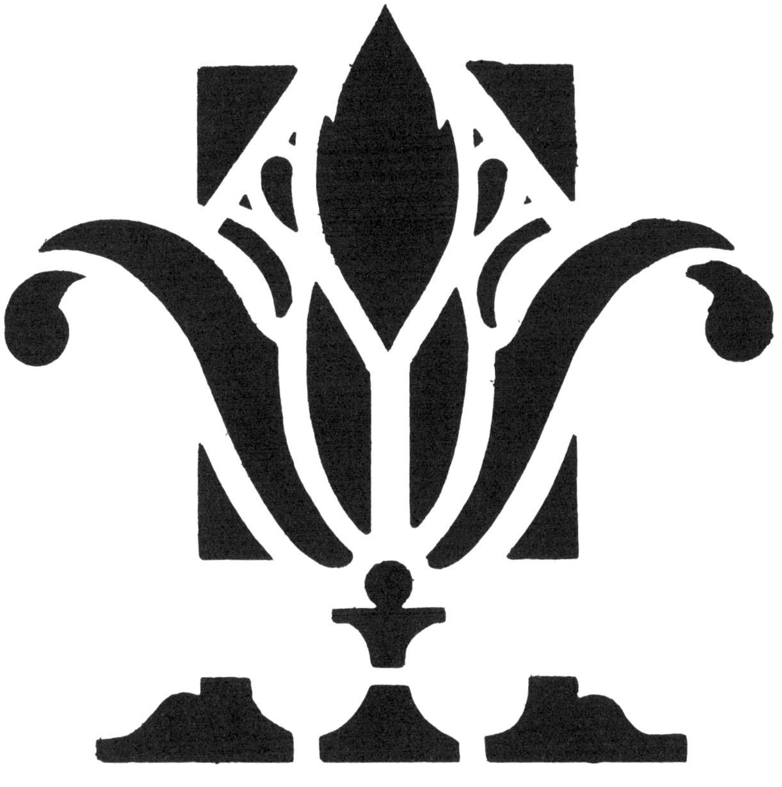

16

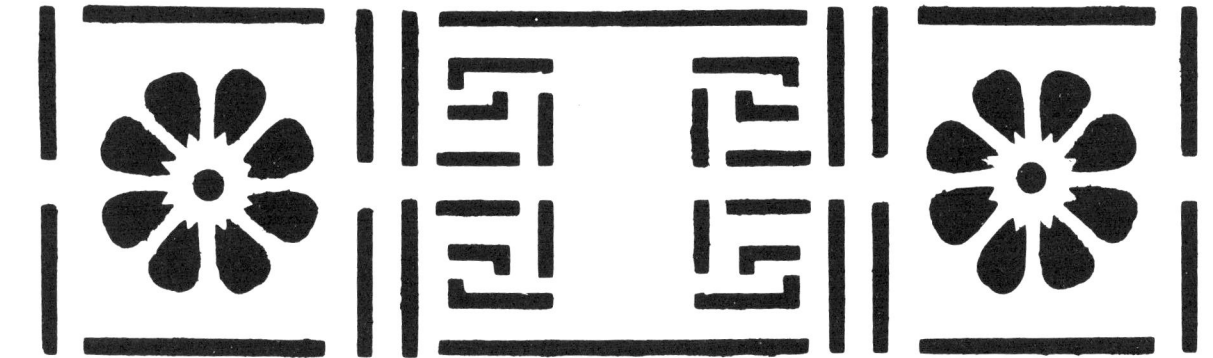

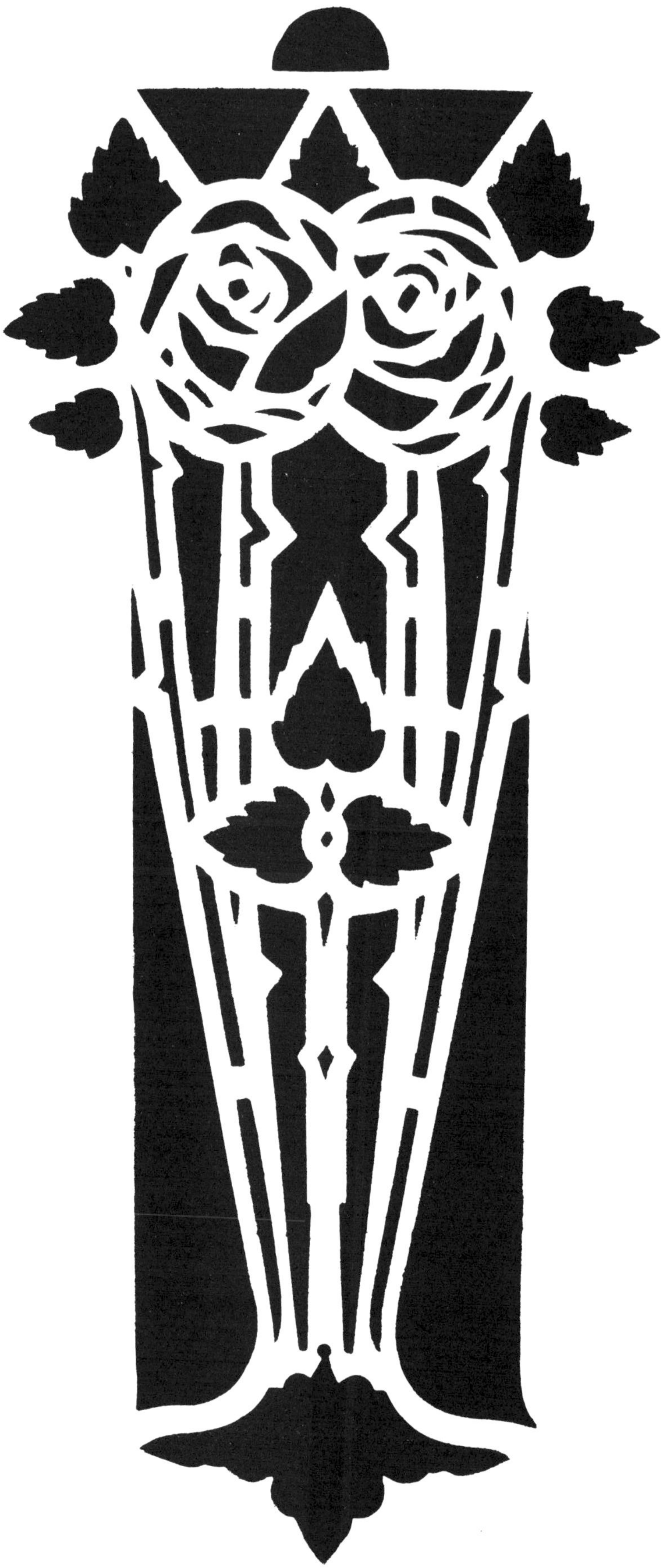

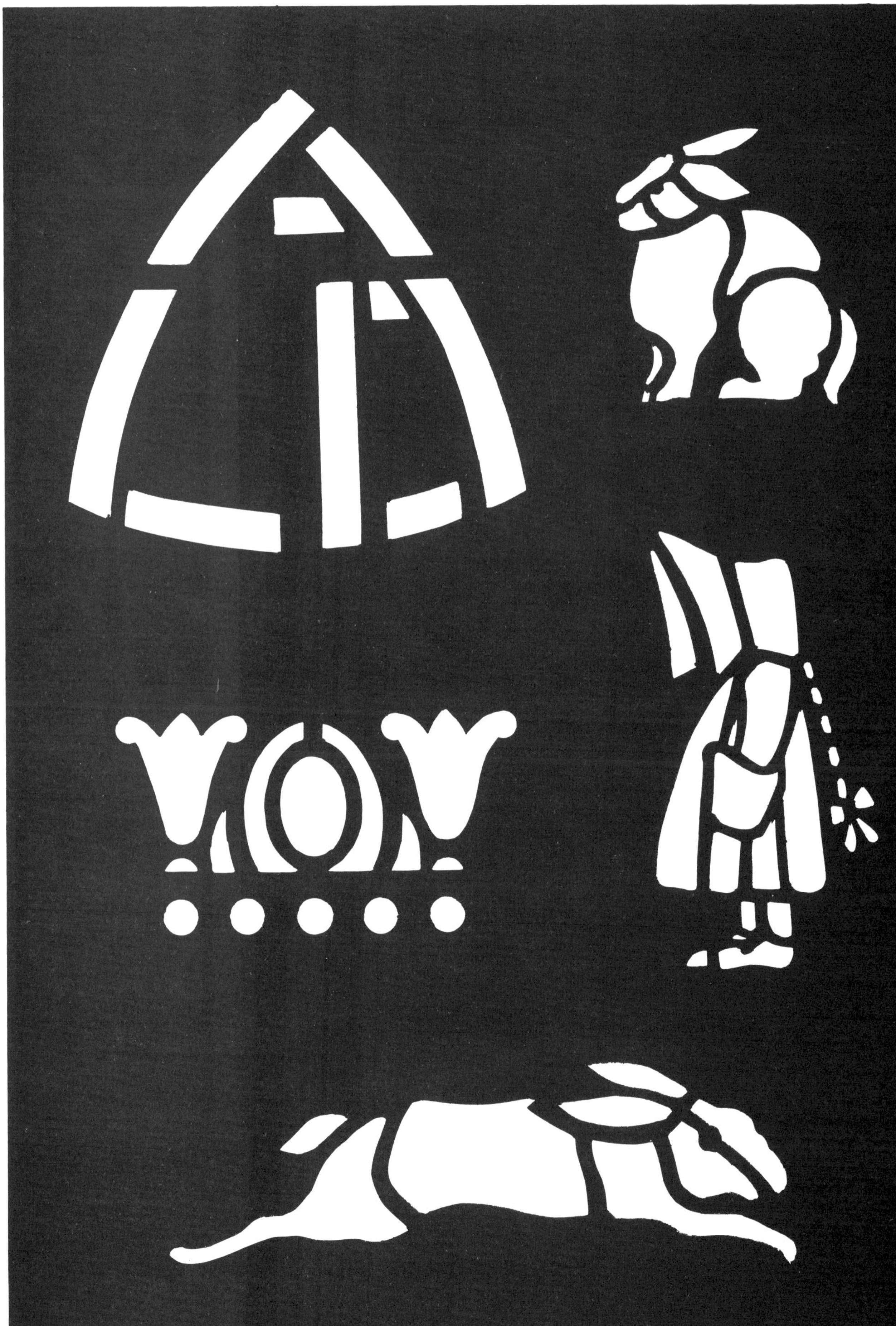

33

34

35

36

37

38

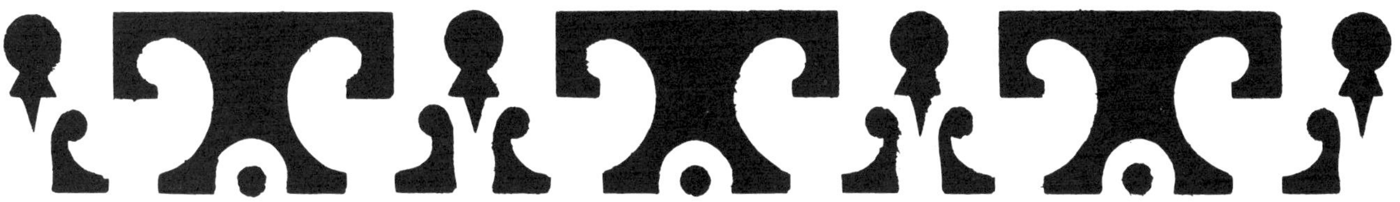

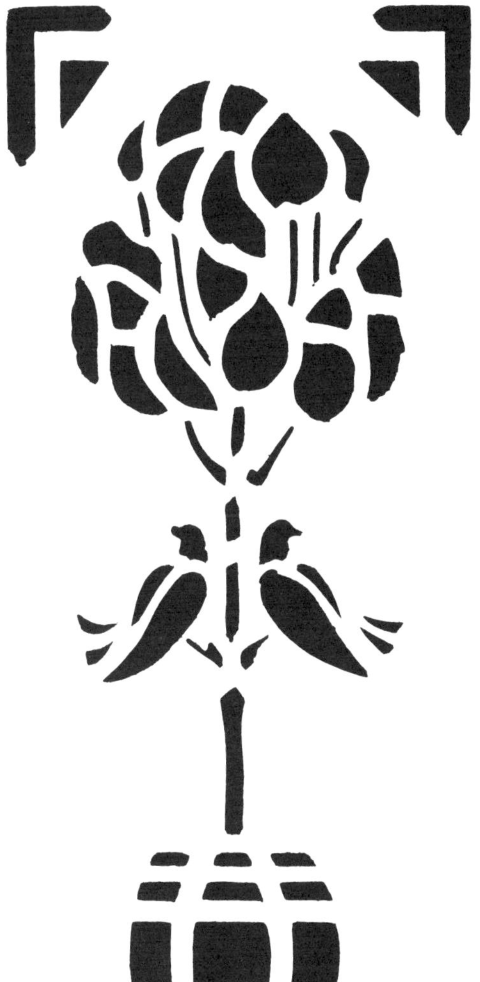

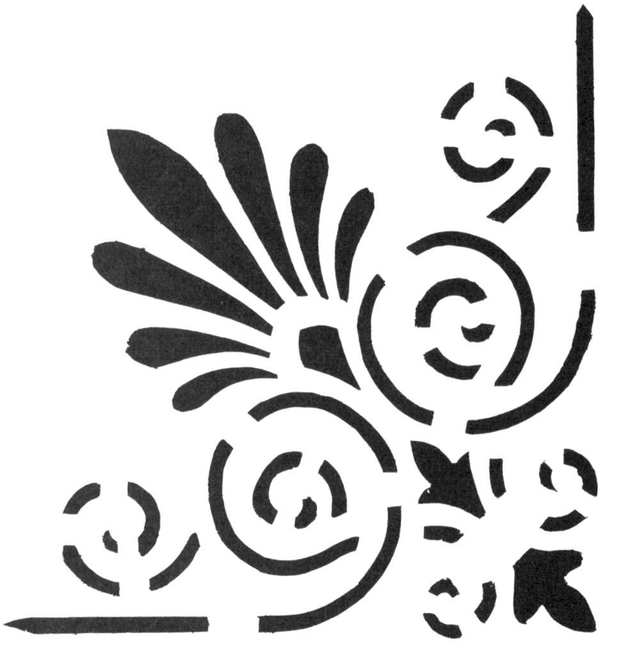

41

42

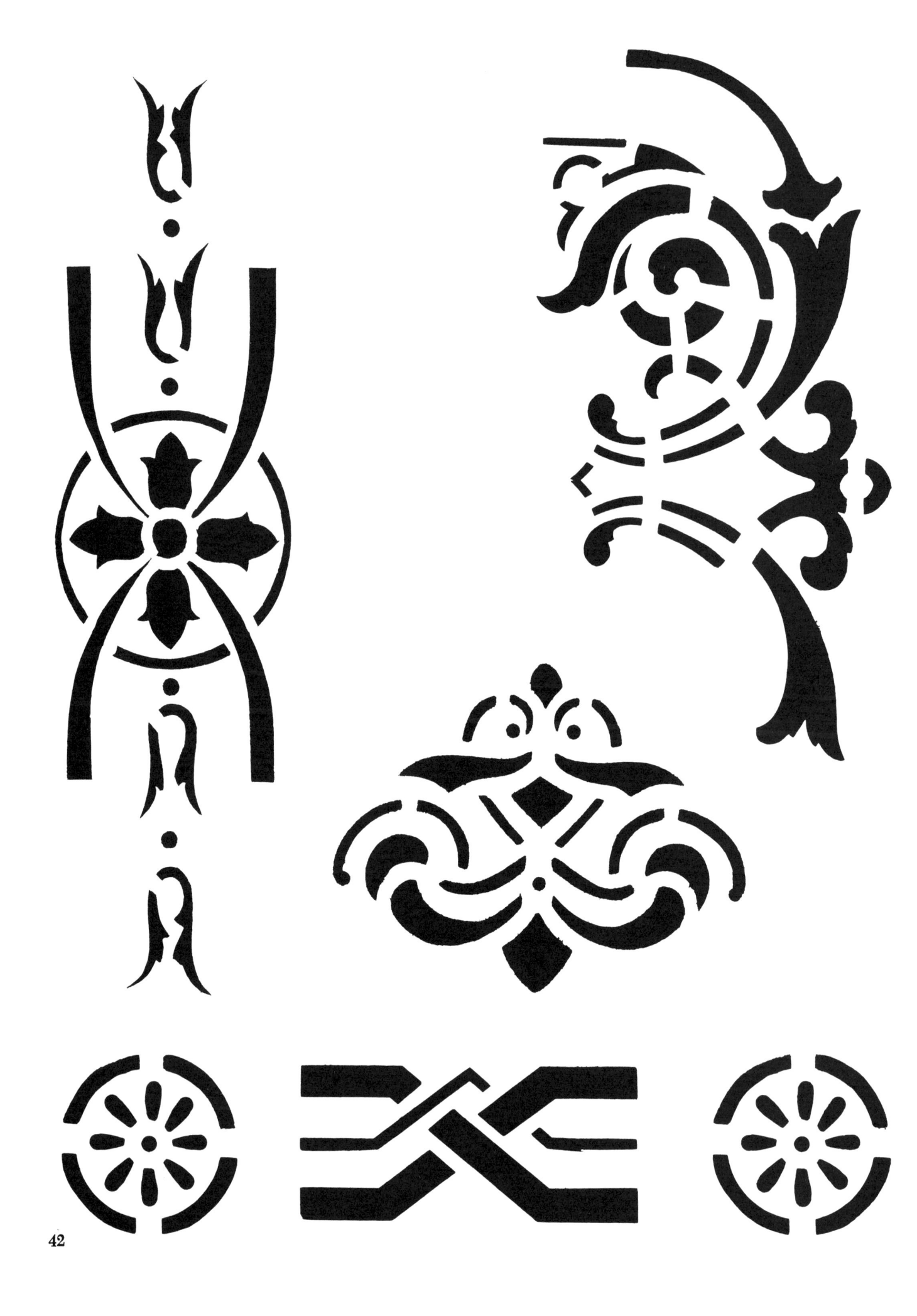

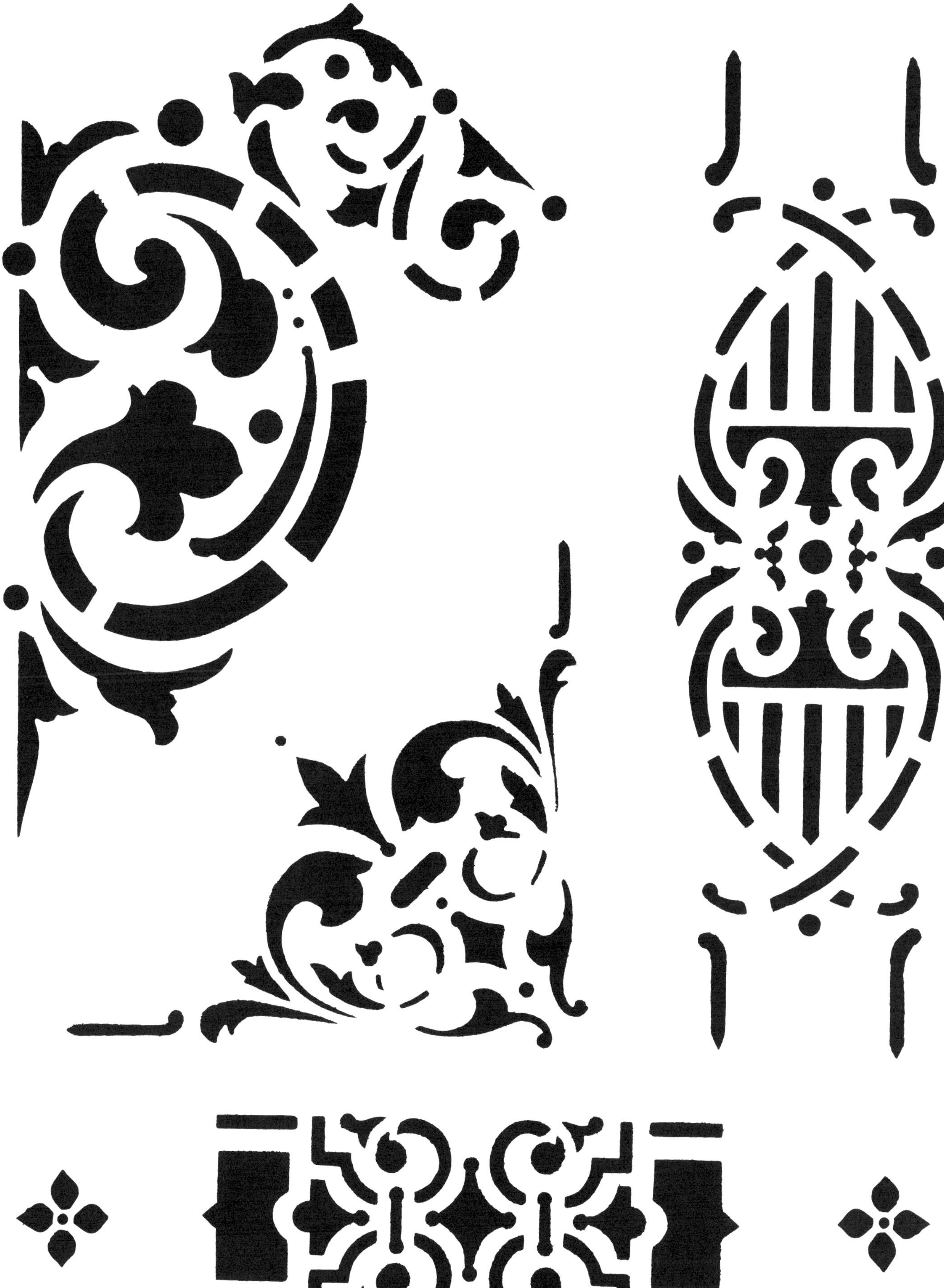

44

47

48

49

50

51

52

53

54

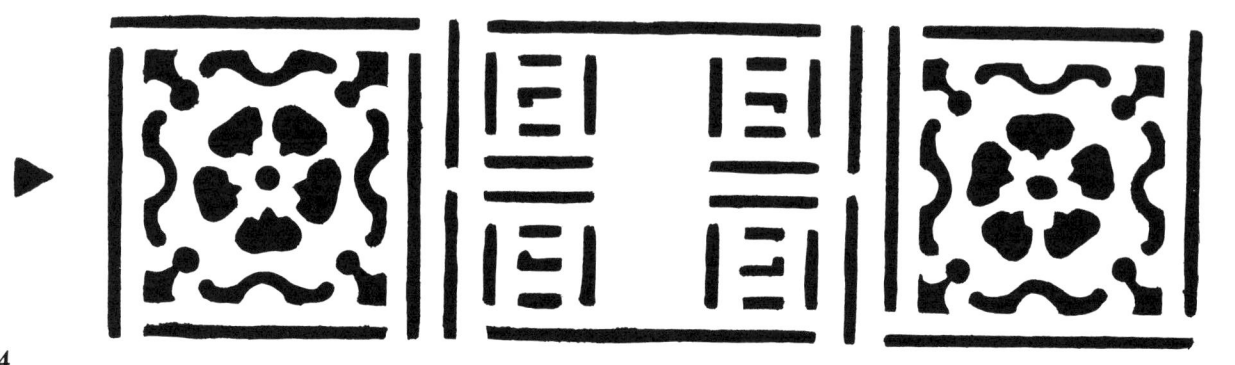

55

56

57

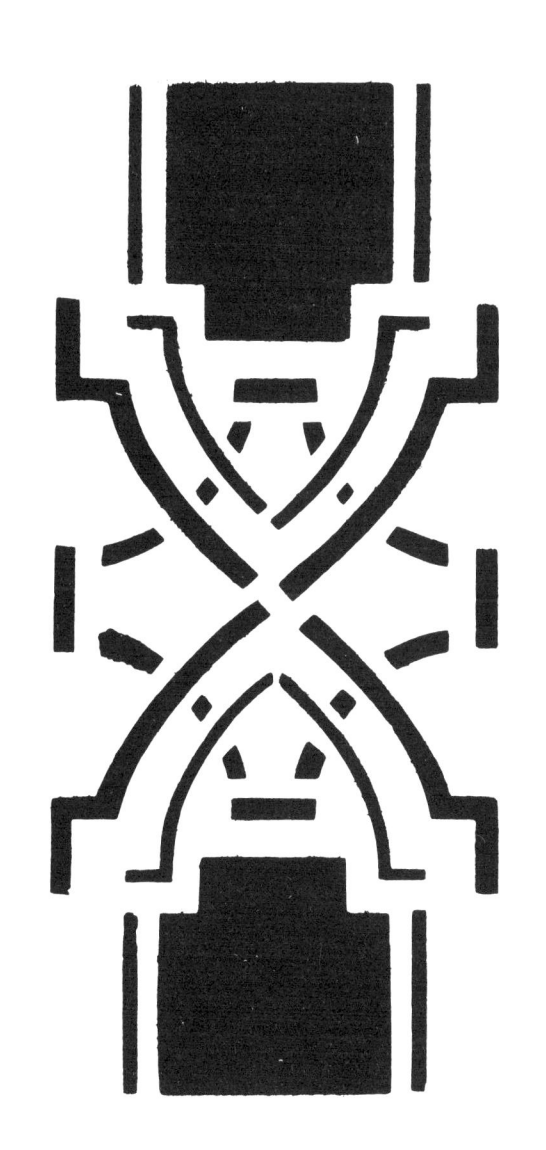

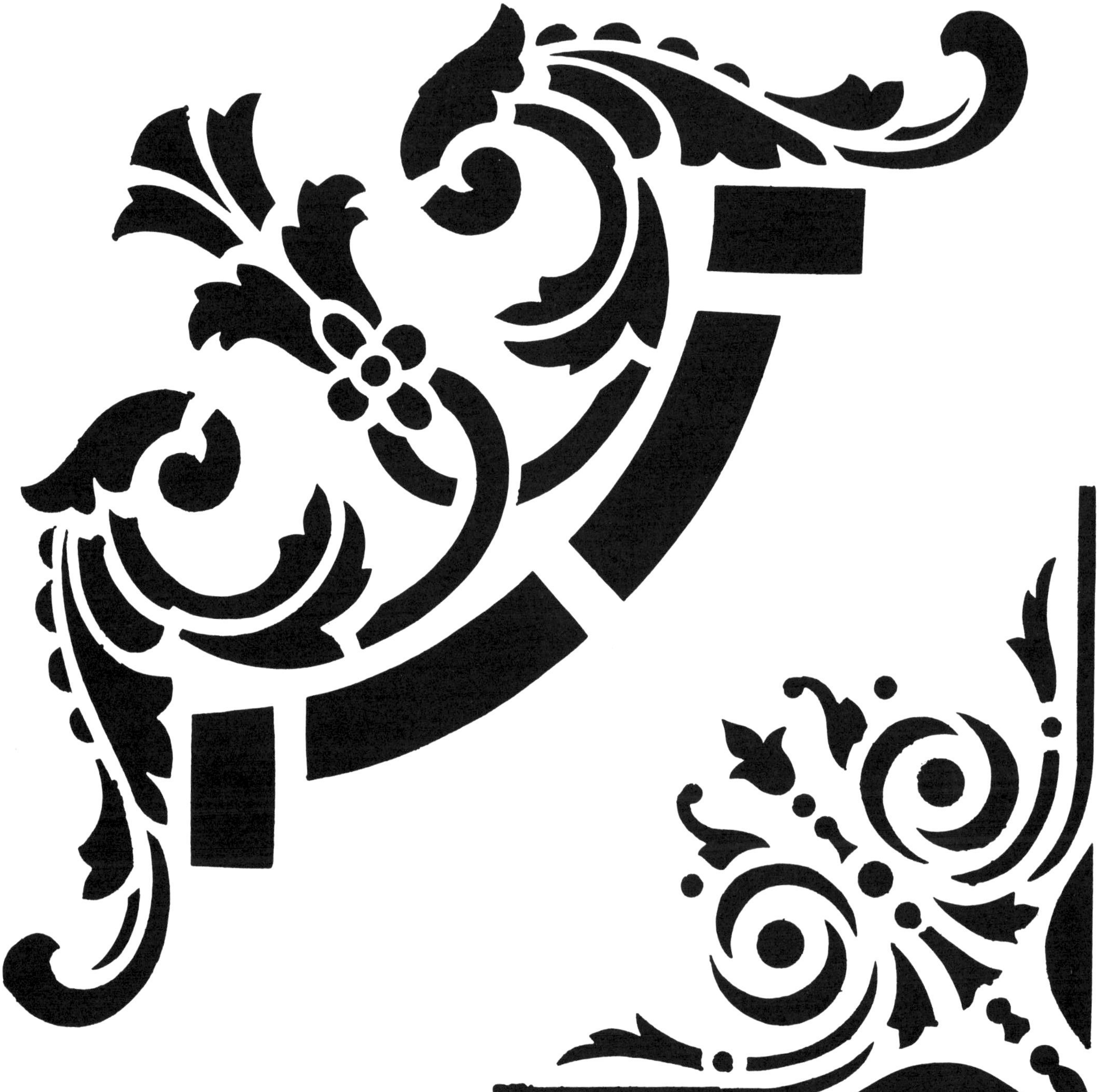

59